ANCIENT CULTURES

Rourke
Educational Media
rourkeeducationalmedia.com

Gary Sprott

WHERE IN THE WORLD?

1 Great Wall of China

2 Great Pyramid of Giza

3 Rome

4 Indus Valley Civilization

5 Incas

6 Nile River

7 Persia

8 Greece

9 Maya

10 Sumerian City of Uruk

11 Aztecs

Table of Contents

Built to Last

Their days of greatness have faded away, but traces of **ancient** cultures are still visible everywhere—even from space! From the French fries you eat to the money in your piggy bank, you just have to look to find fascinating links to the past.

Stretching about 13,000 miles (20,000 kilometers), the Great Wall of China is so big it has been photographed by astronauts. It took nearly 2,000 years to build the wall, a military fortification that kept the Chinese safe from enemy attacks.

The ancient Chinese were not the only people who built to last. The Great Pyramid of Giza was built about 4,500 years ago for the Egyptian king Khufu. The pyramid rose about 480 feet (147 meters) and was made of 2.3 million blocks of stone!

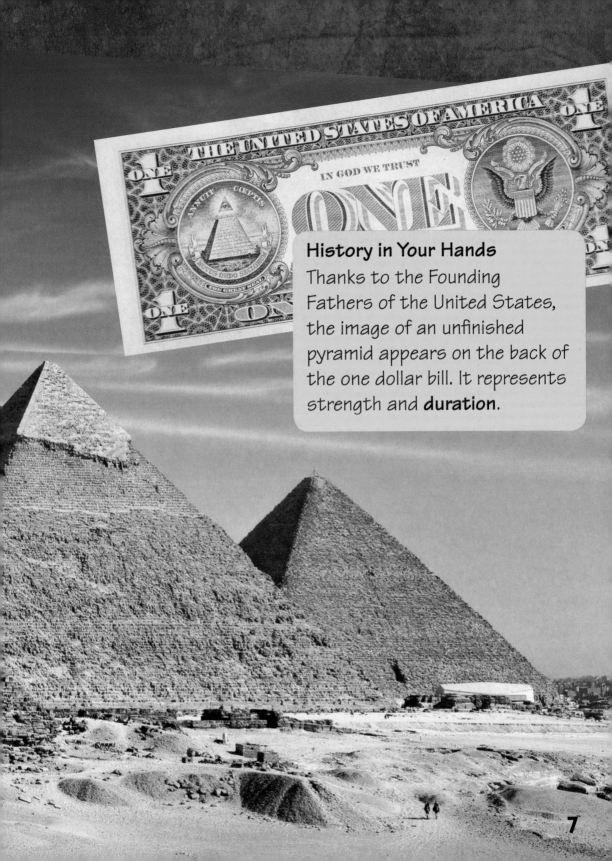

History in Your Hands

Thanks to the Founding Fathers of the United States, the image of an unfinished pyramid appears on the back of the one dollar bill. It represents strength and **duration**.

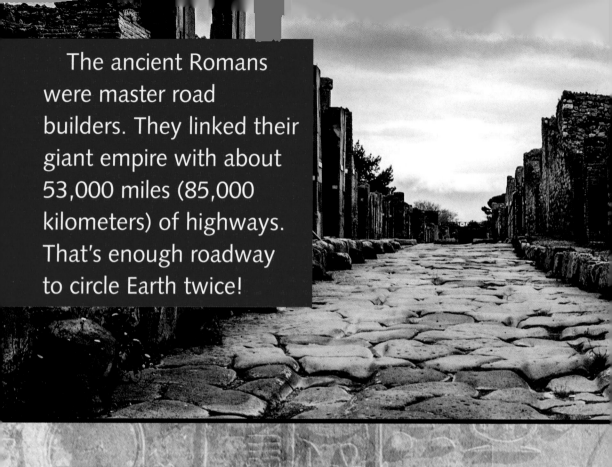

The ancient Romans were master road builders. They linked their giant empire with about 53,000 miles (85,000 kilometers) of highways. That's enough roadway to circle Earth twice!

Ancient Toilets

The Indus Valley Civilization had the first-known flush toilets. But they were toilet holes, not toilet bowls. The toilet was flushed by emptying a jar of water through a clay brick pipe, leading to a drain that fed into a **cesspit**.

Disaster-proof

Inca architecture was built to resist even the strongest earthquakes! The stones vibrate and return to the correct order after a tremor.

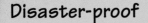

The Incas of South America dug roads through mountains, deserts and forests. They crossed canyons on rope bridges woven from grass and other plants.

Commoners were not allowed to use Inca roads, only government officials. The roads were guarded by soldiers. Trespassers were often killed.

Taste of the Past

Next time you order fries, thank an Inca! They grew potatoes for thousands of years in the Andes Mountains. When the Spanish came to **conquer** Peru, they got a taste for taters and took them back to Europe.

Potatoes were not the only specialty dish of the ancient Incas. Sorry, pet lovers, but the Incas also enjoyed a nice grilled guinea pig. Is it any wonder the furry little creatures always seem so nervous?

That's Nutty!
Ancient Aztecs and Incas invented peanut butter. They roasted the nuts and mashed them into a paste.

The **fertile** lands fed by the Nile River allowed ancient Egyptians to grow many crops. But the main parts of their daily diet were simple: bread and beer!

Wild animals also were hunted by Egyptian rulers. Anything from a hippopotamus to a hedgehog might end up on the royal menu. No need for a toothpick when there's a hedgehog around!

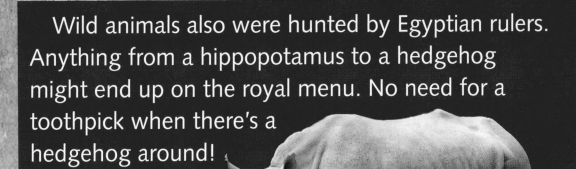

Persians Were Chill

Ancient Persian engineers built coolers called Yakhchal, which were used to store ice and food year-round.

Dinner parties in the Roman Empire were fancy celebrations, but it was still okay to eat with your fingers. (Are you listening, Mom?)

Hey, Give Me Some Elbow Room!
While slaves served them food, guests would lie on their sides and lean on their left elbows. The Roman host gave his most important guest the best couch in the house.

Romans were not afraid to stick their necks out when trying new dishes. Ostrich, anyone? Flamingo tongue and peacock brain might also be served up to impress dinner guests. No wonder they had to lie down!

Animal Kingdoms

For thousands of years, animals have been kept as hunters, protectors, and friends. Cats were considered magical and a source of good luck for their owners.

Furry Friends Go Way Back
Wild cats lived with the people of Mesopotamia more than 100,000 years ago. The felines were domesticated there in about 12,000 BCE, along with goats, sheep, and dogs.

In the homes of rich Egyptian families, cats lived lives fit for a pharaoh. These felines wore jewels and were fed delicious treats. No grumpy cats here!

No Mercy
Ancient Egyptian law dating back to 450 BCE called for the death penalty for anyone who killed a cat.

Caligula, ruler of the Roman Empire, knew how to **pamper** his favorite four-legged friend, Incitatus. The emperor kept his favored horse in a marble stall, where it was fed oats mixed with gold flakes.

Howling at the Moon
Caligula was thought to be more than a little loony. Legend says the emperor rolled around in mounds of money and even talked to the moon!

Dogs were also favored pets in several ancient cultures. Egyptians are credited with inventing the dog collar. Ancient Greeks are credited with inventing the spiked dog collar. The spikes were to protect dogs' throats from animal attacks.

A golden pendant of a dog dating to 3300 BCE was found in the Sumerian city of Uruk.

Home Is Where the Hive Is
Ancient Mayas kept stingless bees as pets! The bees were considered sacred as symbols of Ah-Muzen-Cab, the god of bees and honey. Hives were hung around homes and passed down from generation to generation.

The ancient Chinese calendar marked each new year with the traits of one of 12 animals. Do you like goofing around with your friends? Maybe you were born in the Year of the Monkey!

Rat

Ox

Tiger

Rabbit

Dragon

Snake

Horse

Goat

Monkey

Rooster

Dog

Pig

The animals of the Chinese New Year are the: rat, ox, tiger, rabbit, dragon, snake, horse, goat, monkey, rooster, dog, and pig.

Celebrating with a Bang

Firecrackers were first used in ancient China to scare away evil spirits. Now they are used around the world to celebrate the New Year.

The Chinese New Year, or Spring Festival, is the oldest traditional festival in China.

Strange Sacrifices and Curious Customs

Long before the fairy tale of *Hansel and Gretel*, the Incas were fattening up children to be a **sacrifice** to the mountain gods. The unlucky youngsters were fed llama meat to prepare them for their death. Talk about grim!

The Plomo Mummy is the remains of a sacrificed Incan child. The mummy was discovered on Cerro El Plomo mountain near Santiago, Chile, in 1954.

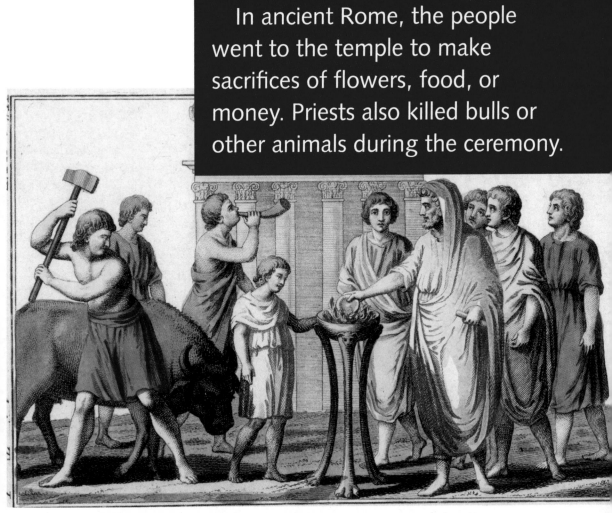

In ancient Rome, the people went to the temple to make sacrifices of flowers, food, or money. Priests also killed bulls or other animals during the ceremony.

Pleasing the Gods

The Romans prayed to gods and goddesses for different reasons. Mars was the god of war and Venus was the goddess of love. Hoping for a big harvest? Saturn was the god for you.

The Romans believed the dead had to cross a **mythical** river by boat so their spirits could reach the underworld. A coin was placed in the dead person's mouth to pay for their journey.

Charon's obol is a term for the coin placed in or on the mouth of a dead person before burial.

Just In Case...
Wealthy Chinese families packed a snack for their loved one's journey to the spirit world. They were buried with large jars filled with food and drink.

Metal masks were placed on the faces of the dead in ancient China. Important people were even buried in suits of bronze or silver to protect their bodies.

Most Inca mummies wore death masks of clay or wood. Members of royal families were dressed to impress in gold death masks.

I Can Still Hear You
Some Inca masks even had parts that moved—including ears!

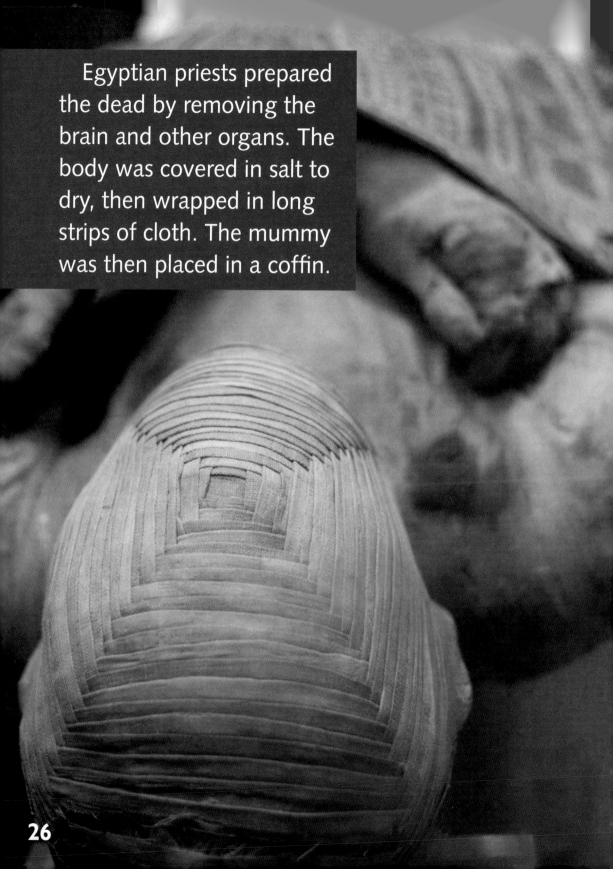

Egyptian priests prepared the dead by removing the brain and other organs. The body was covered in salt to dry, then wrapped in long strips of cloth. The mummy was then placed in a coffin.

Modern-Day Mummies
The ancient Egyptian ritual of mummification was once serious business. Now, it's big business! Mummies are a popular pop culture symbol. They are everywhere, from cartoons and cereal boxes to books, movies, and modern art.

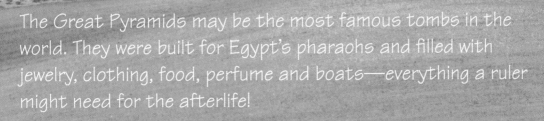

The Great Pyramids may be the most famous tombs in the world. They were built for Egypt's pharaohs and filled with jewelry, clothing, food, perfume and boats—everything a ruler might need for the afterlife!

More...Really Weird, True Facts!

Need stitches? The Mayas used human hair as sutures!

Pre-Columbian Aztecs used cacao beans as money. Want to buy a small rabbit? Thirty cacao beans, please! Even weirder, a father could sell a daughter for 500 cacao beans. Yikes!

Maya also liked for their noses to look like beaks. If nature didn't provide one, they used a removable fake nose bridge to get just the right hook shape.

Ancient Rome had an estimated one million citizens by the first century CE. It would be another 1,800 years before another city—London—passed that number of residents.

The yo-yo was invented by ancient Greeks. It is one of the world's oldest toys.

Ancient Egyptians battled the Hittite Empire for more than 200 years over lands in what is now Syria. In the 1200s BCE, leaders of both empires signed one of the earliest surviving peace treaties. A copy hangs at the entrance of the United Nations Security Council Chamber in New York.

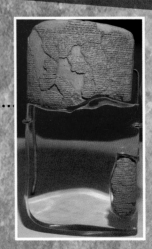

Mayas used to shape their babies' heads to resemble Yum Kaax, the Maize god. Parents flattened their newborn's soft skull by attaching two boards at an angle to press against the forehead so it sloped up and backward. Ouch?!

Though the cause is still a mystery, some experts think Egypt's King Tut was killed by a hippopotamus. The young pharaoh used to hunt them for sport. Scans of Tut show he was buried without his heart and anterior chest wall.

The Aztecs sacrificed humans to keep the sun god happy—according to some estimates, thousands every year. They sacrificed their own people and enemies alike.

Index

Show What You Know

1. Who invented the yo-yo?
2. What did the Incas put on the faces of their dead?
3. What is the oldest traditional festival in China?
4. Who kept bees as pets?
5. Who invented peanut butter?

Glossary

ancient (AYN-shunt): a time long ago

cesspit (SES-pit): a pit for the disposal of liquid waste and sewage

conquer (KONG-kur): to defeat and take control of an enemy

cultures (KUHL-churs): ideas, customs, traditions, and ways of life for groups of people

duration (du-RAY-shuhn): the period of time during which something lasts

fertile (FUR-tuhl): land that is good for growing lots of plants and crops

mythical (MITH-i-kuhl): imaginary or not real

pamper (PAM-pur): to take very good care of yourself or someone else with food, kindness or anything special

sacrifice (SAK-ruh-fise): an offering to a god

Websites to Visit

http://kids.nationalgeographic.com

http://kids.britannica.com

www.si.edu/kids

About the Author

Gary Sprott is a writer and editor in Tampa, Florida. He enjoys reading and spending time with his family. A really weird, totally true fact about Gary is that he really, really likes soccer.

Meet The Author!
www.meetREMauthors.com

www.rourkeeducationalmedia.com

PHOTO CREDITS: Cover and title page: ©Pakpoom, ©gameover2012, ©GlobalP, ©Nerthu2, ©WitR; p.2: ©Nikada, ©Lindrik, ©Rudy Balasko, ©hadynyah, ©siv2203, ©Phototreat, ©naveen0301, ©delihayat, ©JoseIgnacioSoto, Public Domain, ©f9photos; table of contents: ©Jessica Key; p.4-5: ©NI QIN; p.6-7: ©WitR; p.7: ©paulprescott72; p.8: ©zodebala, ©petek arici, ©kakaska; p.9: ©Sandra Kim, ©Serjio74; p.10-11: ©Aleksandr Stennikov; p.10: ©Grafner; p.11: ©GlobalIP, ©Robert Ingelhart; p.13: ©tilo, Wiki; p.14-15: ©National Geographic Creative/Alamy Stock Photo; p.16: ©adogslifephoto; p.17: ©Floortje; p.18: ©Chronicle/Alamy Stock Photo; p.19: Public Doman, ©kwanchaichaiudom; p.20: ©ananaline, ©Delpixart; p.21: ©FUN FUN PHOTO; p.22: Wiki; p.23: ©Mary Evans Picture Library/Alamy Stock Photo; p.24: Public Domain, Wiki; p.25: ©junrong, ©Eduardo Mariano Rivero; p.26: ©Ary6; p.27: ©alexis84; p.28: ©Danny Smythe, ©piccaya, ©Vrabelpeter1; p.29: ©Wiki, ©Dwight Smith

Edited by: Keli Sipperley
Cover design by: Tara Raymo
Interior design by: Rhea Magaro-Wallace

Library of Congress PCN Data

Ancient Cultures / Gary Sprott
(Weird, True Facts)
ISBN 978-1-68342-369-0 (hard cover)
ISBN 978-1-68342-535-9 (e-Book)
Library of Congress Control Number: 2017931261

Rourke Educational Media
Printed in the United States of America,
North Mankato, Minnesota